PULLING THE TRIGGER ON THE AMYGDALA:

DEFINING A POLICE FEAR THRESHOLD

WRITTEN BY

DR. JOHN "JAY" HALL

ABOUT THE AUTHOR

Dr. John Jay" Hall, is a retired lieutenant that served on the Houston Police Department for twenty-three and a half years. Dr. Jay is one of nine children, and the only child who attended a four college. He grew up in Gary, Ind. – Chicago, Ill., and developed his grit from being one of the "corner boys" .With some help from some decent cops, who saw his potential, he was encouraged to go to college. His academic achievements: B.A. Sociology and Criminal Justice from St. Joseph College; M.A. Public Administration from Indiana University NW; M.S.M. in Management from Houston Baptist University; and a PhD in Organizational Behavioral and Management, with a specialization in Leadership from Capella University. He dedicated these accomplishments to his father who only obtained a fourth grade education, but honorably served in the military as did all his brothers with the exception of one. As a baby bloomer, his mental map is still influenced by the civil rights struggle and social justice. He believes in teaching individuals how to fish rather than just giving them a fish. It's part of his tough love campaign for individual growth and social change. His friends call him Jay or John Jay.

ACKNOWLEDGEMENTS

This book is dedicated to all those who came before me and made my journey a little bit easier because of their core values of integrity, fairness, equality, and equity. I would like to personally thank my daughter, Jonquia J. Vaulx, and her husband James, Sr., Little Jay, Jayla, Jayda. Also, I would like to thank the love of my life, Coco, who puts me back together when I get knocked down. I also would like to thank my late parents, "Red" and Mabel Hall for never giving up on any of us. I would like to thank my brothers and sisters for always being there. Here, I would also like to thank my brother in police work and a hell of a detective, Nino Hicks. And, I would also like to thank my three academic sisters, Dr. Jonella Bradford, Dr. Melanie Smith, and Dr. Pamela Webb Redrick. I also want to thank my late grandmother, who always nurtured my spirit in a wholesome way and my cousins Mulch and Stint, who took care of me when I lived in Las Vegas. And finally, I want to thank God Almighty for pruning me spiritually.

TABLE OF CONTENT

CHAPTER ONE   **THE INTRODUCTION**

INTRODUCTION

The purpose of this book is to shift the narrative of police misconduct and the police shooting of minorities from implicit bias to the legal defense narrative of "I was in fear of my life". In the past, attention has been given to the disproportionate number of minorities involved in police related shooting and deaths. Because the shooting are framed in the context of race, both blacks, whites, and police have responded with their own statistics to support their views. Blacks continually point to the disproportionate ratios of blacks to whites in police shooting. In response, whites pointed to a number reflecting that police shoot and kill more whites than blacks. Finally, a third response clarified the debate by citing populations adjustments support the claim that blacks and browns are disproportionately shot more than whites.

This preoccupation with race as the dominant factor in police shooting has added fuel to an already existing fire of police and minority discontent and distrust. The race card when played results in the continuing escalation of each side blaming the other for the problem. Minority citizens blame the police and the police in turn blame the black community for not supporting them. This vicious cycle repeats itself time and time again every time another shooting receives national attention. Is it possible that this race driven narrative that we have created and have endorsed sends a subliminal message that a racial animus explains police misconduct, excessive rights violations, and police shooting? In the recent shooting of Philando Castille, the legal team for Officer Yanez used fear not race. In this case and many others, the officer stated that the actions that he took were a result of his fear. In court, this was the officer's legal defense. It did not justify the shooting based on race, gender, or mental health; rather, it justified the shooting based on the fear held by the officer at that moment.

The absence of race in the legal defense does not diminish the fact that it may have been used to enable the sequence of actions that lead up to the shooting. The role of race can be both a cause and an effect; however, the analysis should not have ended there as some of us understand. Given that race has been used as an explanation for police shooting in lieu of a narrative on fear is somewhat problematic. The discussion on race can be traced to the socio-economic plight of poor people and their historical relationship with the police but the narrative on fear has been lacking equal time. This book makes the assumption that when we frame police misconduct and police shooting on race alone; then, we deliberately prime and misguide the public into thinking that race plays a more dominant role than fear in police shooting.

The aim of this book is to shift the narrative from race alone and to embrace the possibility that determining an officer's fear threshold lends support to determining whether or not the officer has the capacity to do the job. By changing our focus, the issue becomes how can we use neuroscience to determine an officer fittest for duty under pressure and how can we test the officer's fear threshold proactively prior to hiring and periodically after hiring to prevent avoidable police shooting.

CHAPTER TWO   THE PRESENT

This chapter introduces the purpose of the book which begets the question how do we define and determine a fear threshold for police officers. The chapter provides current information on police training academies de-escalation and use of force average course hours. Next, the chapter provides illustrations of three use of force models. The chapter ends by pivoting backward so the reader can place existing de-escalation training and use of force models in their proper social context.

CURRENT POLICE DE-ESCALATION STANDARDS

Despite a number of minority shooting across the country, police training omits fear as a justification of police shooting. As an emotion, fear is a psychological response to one's perceived threats. Police toil in an environment where danger, fear, and uncertainty abound. A recent review of de-escalation and use of force course hours revealed the following:

PERF revealed that academy training allocated an average of 24 training hours for the use of force and 8 training hours for de-escalation training. This review is based on academies across the country. The following breakdown of training instruction hours consist of: Firearms 58; Defensive Tactics 49; Con Law/Legal Issues 40; Basic first aid 16- ; UOF Scenario Based Training 24- ; Communication Skills 10; UOF Policy8 De-escalation 8; Crisis Intervention 8; Baton Techniques 8; ECW 8, and OC Spray 6 (Source: Police Executive Research Forum, 2015).

These training hours represent statistical averages. One limitation of this current material is that the content of the training is not known. A second concern is whether the content of existing training has been validated and recommended as a "best practice". And thirdly, are police departments collecting use of force and shooting data to fine tune their use of force and de-escalation policies. This are issues that fuel an on-going debate between use of force and de-escalation training and officer safety. Below are three illustrations of use of force models:

THREE CURRENT USE OF FORCE CONTINUUM MODELS:

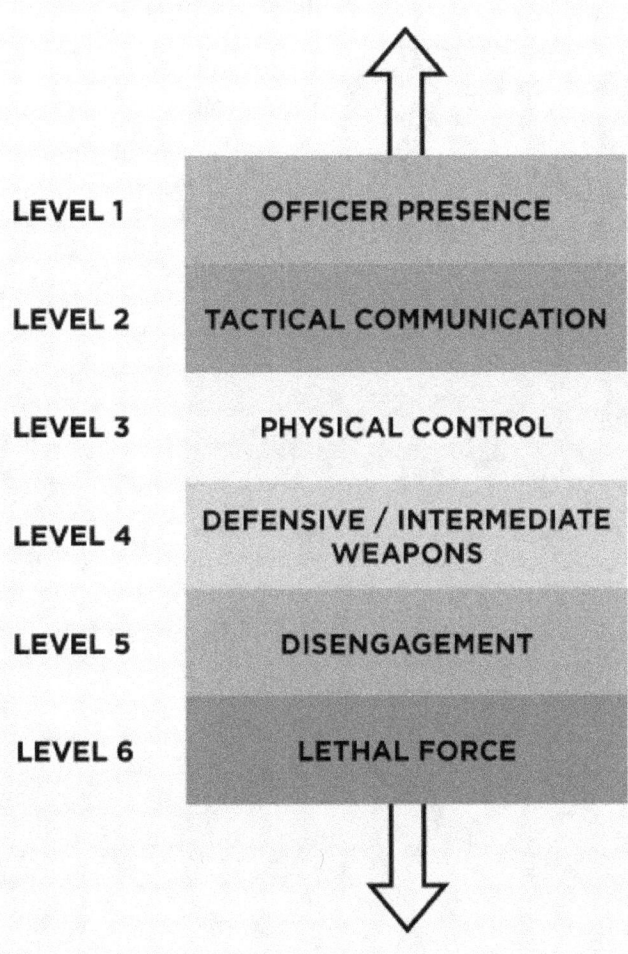

Level Five — Deadly Force — Firearms and Strike to Vital Areas

Level Four — Hard Techniques — Strikes and Takedowns

Level Three — Soft Techniques — Pepper Spray, Come Along & Wrist Locks

Level Two — Verbal Commands — Clear and Deliberate

Level One — Officer Presence — Physical Appearance Professional Bearing

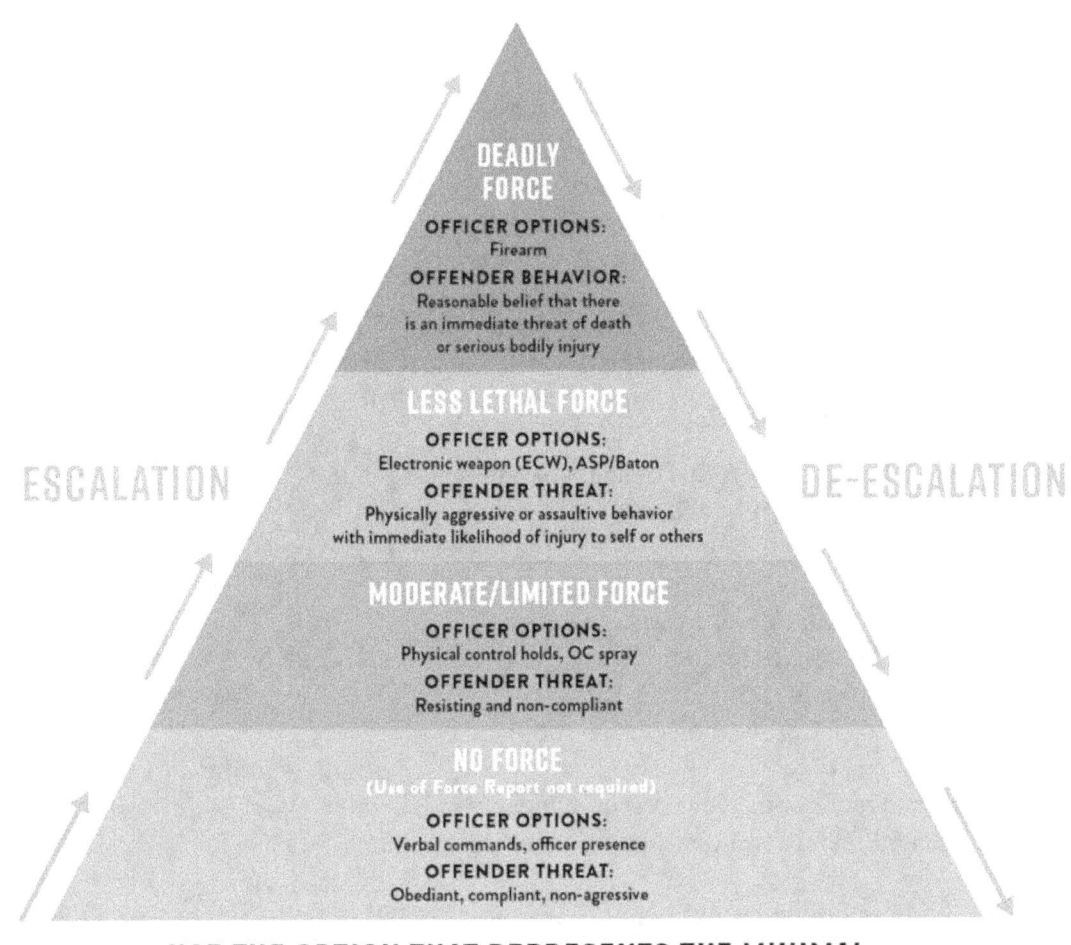

DEADLY FORCE

OFFICER OPTIONS:
Firearm

OFFENDER BEHAVIOR:
Reasonable belief that there
is an immediate threat of death
or serious bodily injury

LESS LETHAL FORCE

OFFICER OPTIONS:
Electronic weapon (ECW), ASP/Baton

OFFENDER THREAT:
Physically aggressive or assaultive behavior
with immediate likelihood of injury to self or others

MODERATE/LIMITED FORCE

OFFICER OPTIONS:
Physical control holds, OC spray

OFFENDER THREAT:
Resisting and non-compliant

NO FORCE
(Use of Force Report not required)

OFFICER OPTIONS:
Verbal commands, officer presence

OFFENDER THREAT:
Obediant, compliant, non-agressive

ESCALATION   DE-ESCALATION

USE THE OPTION THAT REPRESENTS THE MINIMAL
AMOUNT OF FORCE NECCESSARY TO REDUCE THE IMMEDIATE THREAT

Source: Philadelphia Police Department Use of Force Policy, Directive 10.1

In summation, all three models depict a logical sequence of events and the appropriate officer behavior for each event. As with any model, the model represents an approximation of how things should evolve. There is always gap between the police department's espouse theory and their theory in use. This author believes that this gap can be narrowed with proper training and recruitment practices.

DE-ESCALATION POLICIES AND USE OF FORCE

In addition to the three use of force models, the Los Angeles Police Department uses a list of factors that consider the totality of the circumstances that officers should consider in evaluating each situation to determine the appropriate level of force. Below is a list of those factors that an officer should consider. Note: This list is not exhaustive.

(a) The seriousness of the crime or suspected offense;
(b) The level of threat or resistance presented by the subject;
(c) Whether the subject was posing an immediate threat to officers or a danger to the community;
(d) The potential for injury to citizens, officers or subjects;
(e) The risk or apparent attempt by the subject to escape;
(f) The conduct of the subject being confronted (as reasonably perceived by the officer at the time);
(g) The time available to an officer to make a decision;
(h) The availability of other resources;
(i) The training and experience of the officer;
(j) The proximity or access of weapons to the subject;
(k) Officer versus subject factors such as age, size, relative strength, skill level, injury/exhaustion and number officers versus subjects; and,
(l) The environmental factors and/or other exigent circumstances

SOURCE: Los Angeles Police Department (2015)

CHAPTER THREE   **THE PAST**

This chapter begins by providing the socio-economic conditions that impact the behaviors of both the police and citizens. The chapter list poverty, cultural polarization, implicit bias, the legal approach, and disproportionate outcomes as part of the contextual lens that police shooting are viewed from and interpreted from. The chapter ends with a pivot from a narrative on implicit bias to a narrative on the legal approach. And finally, the chapter ends with a narrative of fear as a dominant cause for police shooting and excessive force incidents.

POLICING AND POVERTY

Based upon verifiable statistics, a correlation between high crime neighborhoods, perceptions of fear, and incidents of police misconduct exist. While one of the fundamental core values of police agencies is to reduce fear and to prevent crime, these core values still present a challenge to policing. This author believes that in order to get to the heart of the problem we should reframe the problem to associate crime and police misconduct to *a fear of certain neighborhoods*. By broadening our perspective to include the root causes of socio-economic and political factors that contribute to these impoverished and crime plagued neighborhoods; then, maybe, we can begin to find meaningful solutions that include criminal justice reform that extends beyond traditional police agencies and includes schools, labor markets, housing, welfare, and vocational training. This is a systems approach to policing.

CAUSES OF POVERTY	CONSEQUENCES OF POVERTY
Inappropriate macroeconomics policies	Crime and violence
Unemployment	Area stigma geographic isolation
Lack of education	Ill health and mental health
Lack of employable skills	Child malnutrition
Low wage employment	Social isolation
Infertile land	Sub-standard housing
Poor social and economic intra-structures	Unemployment
Limited access to health care facilities services	Illiteracy
	Teenage pregnancy
	Lack of employable skills
	Emigration

Source: Bowen, G.A. (2003a), Social Funds

By broadening our prospective, the critical public safety issues that we routinely address now can be viewed as part of a much larger social system that is dependent on other social institutions in order to succeed. A systems approach can bring long term goals of fairness, equality, and equity for all individuals.

THE ROLE OF FEAR AND CULTURAL POLARIZATION

Despite the good feelings from songs like, *We Are The World*, there is still a lot of cultural ignorance in the world. Filling this gap requires all of us to put in the work. Our world views are and have been , …… part of our social conditioning. Police officers are no difference. Confronting danger while balancing personal safety and administering civil liberties is no easy task even for the most experience officer. Police have one of the most difficult jobs there is. Unless you are imitating a movie character, such as "Dirty Harry", **I believe all police officers have experienced fear in the course of carrying out their duties**. So the issue becomes, how do police manage fear.

In researching the police culture via my dissertation, A Leadership Perspective on the Police Code of Silence, Procedural Justice, and Police Community Relations, participants described a social process that was both directly and indirectly influenced by an external environment often characterized by danger, fear, and uncertainty. As result of this constructionist study, the following typology of fear was associated with the police code of silence. The finding suggested a typology of behavior that was influenced by fear: (a) fear of making a mistake, (b) fear of field support, (c) fear of management inconsistencies and unfair treatment, (d) fear of retaliation for reporting misconduct, (e) fear of being labeled a snitch, (f) fear of no department protection, (g) fear of being denied transfers and promotions, (h) fear being terminated, (i) fear of lawsuits, and (j) fear of transparency. While the study focused on the police code of silence, it described a **police subculture where fear** replaced trust in a number of situations. The study also reinforced the fact that fear contributed to the "we" versus "them" mindset that characterizes some police and citizen relations. This chasm is widen every time there is a police shooting, especially when the shooting involves a white officer and a black citizen.

The racial overtones have led to a narrative on race and implicit bias.

IMPLICIT BIAS

The narrative on implicit bias is not new. However, pairing it with police shooting and excessive force incidents can be problematic. This pairing of implicit bias with the history of social injustices can imply that a person who manifest an implicit bias has a racial animus toward another race. This is a false narrative. Anyone can hold an implicit bias. As individuals, we learn implicit biases as a result of our societal polarization. If we live in a polarized society; then, our cultural knowledge will be somewhat limited. Fortunately, this deficiency in cultural knowledge can be remedied. However, a person who holds a racial animus may have a belief system that they need to change but refuse to change.

There should be a concern when implicit bias is paired with race and stereotypes. As mentioned, a narrative on police shooting when paired with implicit bias and race has racial overtones. When we say police officers have implicit bias, we are unconsciously saying that disrespectful police encounters, racial profiling, stop and frisk, excessive force, and police shooting can be caused by implicit bias. This explanation may be true to a certain extent but it continues to drive a wedge between the police and citizens. Rather than going down the slippery slope of implicit bias, this author believes that fear offers a better explanation for police misconduct, excessive force, and police shooting.

In employment law, a bona fide occupational qualification is a qualification that employers are allowed to consider when making decisions on the hiring and retention of employees (Wikipedia, 2017). A mandatory retirement age for bus drivers is a safety precaution; therefore, it is acceptable. Implicit bias is not a bona fide occupational qualification for law enforcement; however, fear should be. Can implicit bias explain some police misconduct, excessive use of force, or police shooting…yes, it can. Is it the best answer? No. In the next section, case law is used to explain excessive use of force behavior. Below is an application of the Graham v. Connor (1989) law. This case represents the court's legal standard for determining whether or not an officer's violated their department's use of force standards.

LEGAL APPROACH: USE OF FORCE

Under the Graham v. Connor (1989) law, police shooting and excessive force incidents are explained using the standard of "objective reasonableness". This standard implies that police shooting and excessive forces cases be evaluated based on the world view and the actions most likely taken by other police officers in similar circumstances. Given that police officers are socialized to a culture that is orientated to fear and prone to danger, **officer safety would prevail over any other concerns**.

In the case of County of Los Angeles v. Mendez, (Case №16–369, decided May 30, 2017), the U.S. Supreme Court ("SCOTUS") was asked to decide, among other things, whether a police officer could be held liable for an otherwise **justifiable use of force** on the basis that he committed a separate Fourth Amendment violation that gave rise to the use of force.

On the excessive force claim, the District Court initially said that the deputies acted reasonably in the face of, what they perceived to be, an armed individual in light of *Graham v. Connor*, 490 U.S. 386 (1989)(setting forth the reasonable officer standard). However, the Court, despite saying the officers acted reasonably, went on to hold that the deputies provoked the occasion to use force by unlawfully entering the building, and therefore, found the deputies liable pursuant to the Ninth Circuit's "provocation rule." The Ninth Circuit affirmed in part and reversed in part. Most importantly, the Court affirmed application of the provocation rule.

SCOTUS reversed, holding that the "Fourth Amendment provides no basis for such a rule" (Slip at *syllabus*) and that the rule "is incompatible with [the Court's] excessive force jurisprudence." (Slip at 6). The high court has issued a number of opinions over the last 30 years that have set out, with relative clarity, the standards for judging the reasonableness of a police officer's use of force. Generally speaking, the officer must act in an objectively reasonable manner given the totality of the circumstances. This standard, with *Graham* and it's progeny in mind, is the "settled and exclusive framework for analyzing whether the force used in making a seizure complies with the Fourth Amendment." (*Id.*) In other words, the Ninth Circuit overstepped its authority.

The *Mendez* case is an important one, as it further solidifies what is a remarkably clear set of cases on the use of force. **An officer may use whatever force is objectively reasonable, given the totality of the circumstances and the information known to him at the time of the use of force.** District and Circuit Courts are now reminded of the fundamental framework set in place by cases like *Graham v. Connor* (reasonable officer standard), *Tennessee v. Garner* (weighing government's interests against nature of intrusion into individual rights), *Saucier v. Katz* **(information known to officer at time of use of force)**, *Powpow v. Margate* (shooting of innocent person), *Plakas v. Drinski* (lesser force not required when lethal force justified), and many others, as cited in **Supreme Court Says Cops Justified Even When Provoking A Shooting (2017).**

These cases and their legal reasoning support the necessity of police officer's safety and they should. While case law favors the actions of the police officer, the public is concern with what they see as a pattern of questionable police misconduct in terms of excessive force and police shooting across the country. The following section addresses portions of the public debate over disproportionate outcomes.

DISPROPORTIONATE OUTCOMES

In 2015, The Washington Post launched a real-time database to track fatal police shootings, and the project continues this year. As of Sunday, 1,502 people have been shot and killed by on-duty police officers since Jan. 1, 2015. Of them, 732 were white, and 381 were black (and 382 were of another or unknown race).

But as data scientists and policing experts often note, comparing how many or how often white people are killed by police to how many or how often black people are killed by the police is statistically dubious **unless you first adjust for population**.

According to the most recent census data, there are nearly 160 million more white people in America than there are black people. White people make up roughly 62 percent of the U.S. population but only about 49 percent of those who are killed by police officers. African Americans, however, account for 24 percent of those fatally shot and killed by the police despite being just 13 percent of the U.S. population. As The Post noted in a new analysis published last week, that means black Americans are 2.5 times as likely as white Americans to be shot and killed by police officers.

U.S. police officers have shot and killed the exact same number of unarmed white people as they have unarmed black people: 50 each. But because the white population is approximately five times larger than the black population, that means unarmed black Americans were five times as likely as unarmed white Americans to be shot and killed by a police officer.

[Unarmed and black: Police are still killing unarmed black men at higher rates than whites]

Police have shot and killed a young black man (ages 18 to 29) — such as Michael Brown in Ferguson, Mo. —175 times since January 2015; 24 of them were unarmed. Over that same period, police have shot and killed 172 young white men, 18 of whom were unarmed. Once again, while in raw numbers there were similar totals of white and black victims, blacks were killed at rates disproportionate to their percentage of the U.S. population. Of all of the unarmed people shot and killed by police in 2015, 40 percent of them were black men, even though black men make up just 6 percent of the nation's population.

And, when considering shootings confined within a single race, a black person shot and killed by police is more likely to have been unarmed than a white person. About 13 percent of all black people who have been fatally shot by police since January 2015 were unarmed, compared with 7 percent of all white people, as cited in (Lowery, 2016).

The concerns held by the public regarding disproportionate outcomes have been addressed via town hall meeting across the country. A number of recommendations have been offered. The verdict on these recommendations and the results of these change strategies are still out. However, the public is doubtful that any changes will take place. The disproportionate number of minority police shooting in comparison to whites shot by the police has fueled a perceived narrative that police shooting of minorities are explained in terms of a racial animus. The pairing of disproportionate outcomes and race has led to an *unintentional conditioning* of the public that the police do not administer the law in a fair and impartial manner. In addition to questions about fairness, the disproportionate outcomes also raise concerns about whether the police can police its own. Suggesting the need for an independent civilian review board with subpoena power. In the previous sections, questionable police actions have been explained in terms of sociology (implicit bias) and the law (legal cases), the next section includes the *perspective of the officer engaged in the shooting.*

SHIFTING FROM IMPLICIT BIAS, TO LEGAL, TO FEAR

As presented in the previous section, police shooting have been defined within both a sociological context and a legal context. And for the most parts, these explanations have been offered to explain an institutional point of view. In this section, the following incidents represent the perspectives of the first responders. In each of these incidents and in many others, fear was the motive behind an officer's decision to act.

INCIDENT I. THE FEAR DEFENSE: POLICE SHOOTING

Within the ongoing story about race and killings by police there has been, from the beginning, a second story, about fear. For the shooters themselves, fear has been essential to their legal defense; it has also been, in a more basic way, their explanation. The situation was pressured; they could not control the person in front of them; violence seemed imminent and they were scared.

Sometimes the shooters have seemed less specifically scared of the suspect than generally alarmed by their environment. "When you fear for you and your partner's safety, you would take your weapon out," Peter Liang, the rookie cop who killed Akai Gurley when he fired blindly into a dark stairwell in an East New York housing project, told the jury. "When approaching these areas, I feel I need to take my gun out."

The Harvard economist Roland Fryer published an examination of racial bias in police shootings that was immediately understood to be both important and controversial. He could detect racial bias in nearly every type of encounter that police had with citizens. They were more likely to stop African-Americans than white citizens. In those stops, officers were more likely to draw their guns when the suspect was black, and once the weapon was drawn, they were more likely to point it at someone who was African-American. Blacks were more likely to get handcuffed, thrown against a wall, and pushed down. The racial discrepancy, controlling for circumstance, was present in nearly every situation.

The exception was the most severe form of police force—shootings. There, Fryer's team could find no racial bias at all.

Fryer's study, the data journalist Mona Chalabi concluded, in the *Guardian*, was "not indicative of a wider picture."

But Fryer's account, in making distinctions between the different situations in which officers find themselves, offers something other than the wider picture: insight into the elements of fear, and their interaction with racial bias. Consider the emotional conditions. When an officer stops a citizen, he is entirely in control of the situation. When he handcuffs a suspect, or hurls him into a wall, he is perhaps only a little less so. When he draws his gun and points it at the ground, he recognizes that a danger is present but not acute; he is focused on alleviating the possibility of violence. When he raises his weapon and points it, he believes that the possibility of violence is acute but not imminent. As the situation escalates, his own fear and stress are rising, his own sense of control slipping away. When he decides to shoot, he has lost control of the situation. His fear and stress are at their maximum. It is at this point when we expect him to act the most, because the pressure on his own control is so intense, because he is acting without thinking. And yet, if Fryer is right, this is precisely the moment when racial bias disappears, and where the officer perceives a white suspect to be as much a threat as a black one. The implication is that racial bias in these situations works differently than we had thought.

The fear defense, when it is offered by shooters, uses emotion and irrationality as a shield, to deflect attention from the bias beneath. But if Fryer's results are to be believed, then it is hard to argue that racial bias emerges in the most extreme circumstances into which we send the police. Police bias no longer looks like a problem of instinctive reaction, but of voluntary action. The emphasis shifts, away from the moment when shots are fired, and toward all the decisions that led to that point. If Fryer is right, then the whole phenomenon of police racial bias loses its shield of emotion and instinctual heat, and looks like a much colder operation.

SOURCE: Benjamin Wallace-Wells (July 12, 2016), New Yorker / Harvard Researcher/ fear

---

INCIDENT II. CHICAGO COP'S DEFENSE IN MURDER CASE DEPENDS ON HIS FEARS, EXTENT OF THREAT

By Joseph Ax and Tom Polansek | NEW YORK/CHICAGO

NEW YORK/CHICAGO The murder case against a white Chicago police officer for killing a black teenager may turn on whether the officer can show that he feared for his life and that firing 16 times was reasonable under the circumstances, criminal defense experts said.

Officer Jason Van Dyke is accused of shooting 17-year-old Laquan McDonald just six seconds after emerging from his patrol car on a street on the southwest side of Chicago on Oct. 20, 2014, emptying his gun's clip. A graphic video of the killing, captured by a patrol car camera, was released publicly on Tuesday night, 13 months after the shooting.

According to Greene, the core question is: "What did he do that placed you in reasonable apprehension of death or serious bodily injury?"

But even if he can persuade a jury or judge he believed his life was in jeopardy, Van Dyke could still face conviction if his fear is found to have been unreasonable.

Appearing on CNN on Wednesday, Van Dyke's attorney Daniel Herbert said the officer "truly was in fear for his life as well as the lives of his fellow police officers."

SOURCE: Ax and Polansek (Nov. 25, 2015), Chicago cop's defense in murder case depends on his fears, extent of threat. Reuters

INCIDENT III. WHITE ST. LOUIS POLICE OFFICER SHOOTS OFF-DUTY BLACK OFFICER

ST LOUIS – A black off-duty St. Louis police officer was shot by a white on-duty police officer from the same department who apparently mistook him for a fleeing suspect, according to a statement from the St. Louis Metropolitan Police Department.

At about 10 p.m. Wednesday evening, St. Louis police received a report that a stolen vehicle had been spotted. Officers laid down spike strips and turned on their lights, but the occupants of the vehicle allegedly opened fire on police. Officers followed the car until it crashed.

According to the police statement, the armed suspects then fled on foot. Meanwhile, an off-duty officer who lived near where the crash occurred came outside with his department issued firearm after hearing the commotion.

Two officers "challenged the off-duty officer and ordered him to the ground," the department said. The officer complied and once they recognized him the on-duty officers told him "to stand up and walk toward them."

Implementing police body cameras remains work in progress
The New York Police Department is implementing the country's largest body camera program. More than 20,000 officers will wear the cameras once th...

At about the same time, another officer who had just arrived on the scene saw what was happening and "fearing for his safety and apparently not recognizing the off-duty officer, discharged a shot, striking the off-duty officer in the arm."

The injured officer was taken to the hospital and has since been released. He is described as 38 year old with 11 years of service. The department says that the officer who allegedly shot him is 36 years old with over eight years of service. Two of the three suspects in the stolen car chase were taken into custody and booked on $500,000 cash bond. One suspect is still at large. Seven officers have been placed on administrative leave while the shooting is investigated (Crimesider, 2017).

INCIDENT IV. CHICAGO DETECTIVE SHOT 28 TIMES, LIVES. SENTENCED TO 40 YEARS IN PRISON.

This next case involves a black Chicago railroad Detective shot by four whites Chicago Police in 2005. The following incident describes the news account of what transpired:

Howard Morgan, a retired officer of the <u>Chicago Police Department</u>, was shot 28 times by four active Chicago police officers: John Wrigley, Eric White, Timothy Finley and Nicolas Olsen. Morgan was accused of aggravated battery, discharging a firearm, and attempted murder; no charges were filed against the police officers.

Morgan was driving home from his job as senior patrolman at the railroad. Around 12:45 AM on February 21, Chicago police officers John Wrigley and Timothy Finley pulled him over— for driving the wrong way on a one-way street and for having his lights off; they were joined by Officers Nicolas Olsen and Eric White. The events which followed are in dispute.

Morgan says he was pulled from his vehicle by the four officers, who restrained him as he sought to produce police identification. He says one of the officers found his gun (a Glock 9mm), shouted "gun!," and removed the gun from Morgan's waistband. Next came a wave of shooting.

According to the officers, Finley saw Morgan pull out his gun. Finley yelled to the other three. Morgan fired seventeen gunshots, hitting Olsen's upper right arm, White's right calf, and Wrigley's left arm. Charice Rush, the only testifying third party witness at the scene, said she saw the officers 'snatch' Morgan from his van and force him onto one knee. She overheard an officer say "Oh shit, he has a gun." Rush said she saw the four officers open fire on Morgan while he lay on the ground. Morgan was reported as having been shot 25 times. By the end of Morgan's 2007 trial, this number had been revised to 28. In addition to the 28 bullets that hit Morgan, many more were shot into the air, into Morgan's van, and into the walls and furniture of nearby houses.

He was transported to Mt. Sinai hospital where his condition was reported as critical. According to Phillip Zaret, the trauma surgeon who treated on Morgan that night, Morgan had injuries to his neck, back, leg, liver, kidney, and colon. Dr. Zaret also treated Olsen for the wound to his arm. Morgan took 7 months to recover.

Morgan was found not guilty of battery or discharging a firearm in his 2007 trial; no verdict was returned on attempted murder. Morgan was tried a second time for attempted murder and convicted in January 2012. In April 2012, he was sentenced to 40 years in prison. His case drew outrage from activists within Chicago and around the country. In January 2015, departing Illinois governor Pat Quinn granted him clemency (Wikipedia.org/Wiki/Howard_Morgan_case, 2005).

Within each of the above shooting incidents, the common thread explained by officers or their attorneys was that their clients were in fear of their lives. This narrative of fear or the generalization of fear as an explanation is *problematic* because the explanation whether justified or not can be cited every time there is a police shooting. Current procedural safeguards don't seem to prevent such a generalized use. Fear can be construed as in the eye of the beholder. And if so, how do we manage fear when it depends on the subjective experiences and interpretations of every individual officer? Should police administrators consider the **ability to manage fear as a bono fide occupational qualification?** And, if so, what levels are considered acceptable and under what circumstances? Determining an officer's ability to cope and manage fear on the job should be determined before they are hired and periodically doing their employment. *Defining and developing a fear threshold standard may require a different kind of training and a different kind of research.*

With respect to training, the President Obama Task Force (2015) listed the following strategies to improve police community relations. These strategies included: community policing, interpersonal skills, communication skills, bias awareness, scenario based training, crisis intervention, procedural justice and impartial policing, mental health training, analytical research, and cultural responsiveness. Some of these same training recommendations were contained in the body of my dissertation (2015) which I shared with NOBLE and various members of the Obama Task Force on 21st Century Policing. Yet, despite the above training, this author believes that the disproportionate number of minority shootings have not been adequately explained.

This author believes that you cannot change the police culture without changing the police mindset. Shifting the police mindset requires more than creative writing. It requires different tools and different skill sets in order to narrow the gap between the organization's *espouse theories* (policies, procedures and practices) and their *theories in use* (the way the organization really does things). This author believes shifting the current police mindset from the *Warrior mind set* to what Obama Task Force referred to as a *Guardian mind set* requires a complete understanding of how the brain works in its survival mode. The next section deals with fear and how the brain works in its' survival model. The chapter lays the groundwork for the need to incorporate neuroscience research within de-escalation and use of force training.

CHAPTER FOUR   THE FUTURE

This chapter attempts to move the dialogue forward to embracing the importance of neuroscience in understanding the Warrior mindset, police shooting, and the excessive uses of force. This author believes managing fear is a bona fide occupational qualification because police must be able to manage certain levels of fear in order to do their jobs in a manner that is acceptable to the public. The failure of an officer to control and manage his or her emotions can result in and will continue to result in shooting that may be avoidable. The following chapter discusses how the brain works, the functions of the right and left brain, the amygdala, an amygdala hijack, the sympathetic nervous system, retooling the shoot, don't shoot exercise, neuroscience research, and holistic training strategies. The chapter concludes with the suggestions for police to utilize neuroscience in their de-escalation and their use of force training practices.

UNDERSTANDING THE BRAIN

The brain is a remarkable creation by God. It has been said by various researchers that the brain processes anywhere from 50,000 to 70,000 thoughts a day and has 100 billion brain cells. However, scientist have discovered that the human brain is not based solely on logic. Menkes (2005) stated that a **new theory of connectionism** has emerged to explain how the brain works. "The brain is able to perform as many as two hundred trillion operations in a second not serially but simultaneously and allows vast amounts of knowledge to be brought to bear on a decision all at once" p. 111. The brain can instantly access information from previous experience that seems relevant to the problem at hand. The mind can thrive on imperfect information; it can generalize and fill in missing parts from its large reserves of worldly knowledge, with plausible guesses and fast approximations (Menkes, p.111). This process often masquerades as logical reasoning. Previous experiences become our substitute for "rational" thought, as the human brain recognizes answers to (past) problems rather than deducting them from facts. Human memory cannot help but to connect things that seem familiar (Menkes, 2005, p.111). This information reinforces that humans have limited knowledge based on their particular experiences and they engage in a process of sense making which compensates for the gaps in their knowledge and experiences.

This information also implies that the brain stores and recalls your emotional experiences as well. The fact that the brain retrieves the emotions attached to your emotional experiences implies that your emotions that are associated with a certain event don't change unless your experiences change. In one research study on Holocaust survivors, Rachel Yehuda (2015) discovered that the signs of the trauma experienced by the parents were passed along to their children based on chemicals attaching to the parent's DNA. This process is called "epigenetic inheritance" and it occurs when environment influences such as smoking, diet, and stress can through chemical re-engineering affect the genes of your children or grandchildren (Thomson, 2015). Assuming that we pass not only our physical DNA traits to our children, but also our emotional DNA may be helpful in understanding how our environments influence our behaviors.

UNDERSTANDING THE REPTILIAN BRAIN

Our need to respond to threats in the environment was by design. The need for fast responses drew out of our need for survival. Our ancestors did not have the time to calculate a complex problem when threaten. As part of our development, our brain was hard wired to response to threatening situations with a freeze, fight or flight response. This hard wiring has not changed today. We still have a tendency to think fast. Unfortunately, in a complex world, fast decisions can be a hindrance (Menkes, 2005). According to Jeremy Campbell (1990), The Improbable Machine, logic follows a careful, wholly consistent sequence of rules; a contradiction in any part of the sequence causes the whole system to crumble. Logic cannot tolerate inconsistency or significant gaps in knowledge (Menkes, 2005, p.109). The human brain has evolved to function in an environment that is both complex and full of contradictions. Therefore, Menkes, as well as others, believe that *the brain does not operate in a logical sense as we once presumed*. In fact, Menkes, stated, "the human brain is consistently, systematically illogical" as cited in (Revlin et el, 1980). Because humans have a limited capacity with respect to their knowledge based on their experiences only, they employ a process called *sense making* to fill in the gaps. Unfortunately, sense making can results in projecting our understanding on others even when our understanding are inaccurate. Understanding how the brain works is crucial in developing use of force and de-escalation training because our thinking are a representation of our experiences. Our experiences shape our assumptions and world view. This is a critical piece of information when we are trying to assess or to determine the intentions of others with respect to whether or not they are trying to harm us. Understanding how the brain functions helps us to better understand how we formulate our beliefs and better manage our emotions.

LEFT BRAIN/RIGHT BRAIN, SLOW BRAIN/FAST BRAIN

As we know it, the brain is composed of a left and right hemisphere. Each performs a different set of functions. Some researchers have stated that the left hemisphere has 186 million more neurons than the right hemisphere. A plausible explanation for this vast different may be attributed to a point made by Charmine (2015) that Westerns use the left brain more than the right brain. The chart below highlights some of the functions of the right and left brain.

LEFT BRAIN FUNCTIONS	RIGHT BRAIN FUNCTIONS
Small Picture	Big Picture
Verbal Communication	Nonverbal Communication
Small Muscle Control	Large Muscle Control
Intelligence Quotient	Emotional Quotient
Word Reading	Comprehension
Math Calculations	Math Reasoning
Processing Information	Interpreting Information
Conscious Actions	Unconscious Actions
Positive Emotions	Negative Emotions
Receiving Auditory Input	Interpreting Auditory Input
Linear and Logical Thinking	Gets Abstract Concepts
Curious and Impulsive Actions	Cautious and Safe Actions
Like Routine/Sameness	Likes Newness, Novelty
Activates Immunity	Suppresses Immunity

In his most recent book, Daniel Kahneman (2011) also describe the brain as having two functions for decision making. However, he coined different terms for how the brain functions. He labelled the two functions as System 1 thinking and System 2 thinking. System 1 thinking was characterized as fast thinking and System 2 was characterized as slow thinking. The dominant characteristic of System 1 thinking was that it was automatic, intuitive, and unconscious. On the other hand, System 2 thinking was more control oriented, focused, effortful, and attentive requiring greater mental concentration. Kahneman stated that System 1 thinking works by using the individual's associative memory to interpret what going on. The associative memory works by pairing certain words and ideas. Kahneman implied that these two systems work in tandem; however, System 2 Thinking is used to verify facts, ideals, and events presented by System 1 Thinking. Another neuroscientist, Epstein (1994) described the same functions using the terms experimental thinking and rational thinking. Epstein's experimental thinking was similar to system 1 or fast thinking, as cited in Kahneman.

CHARACTERISTICS OF SYSTEM ONE THINKING:

Below are some characteristics of System 1 Thinking:

Generates impressions, feelings, and inclinations, when endorsed by System 2

Operates automatically and quickly with no sense of voluntary control
Can be programmed by System 2 when a pattern is detected
Executes skilled responses and generates skilled intuitions after adequate training
Creates a coherent pattern of activated ideas in **associative memory**
Distinguishes the surprising from the normal
Infers and invents causes and intentions
Is bias
Exaggerates emotional consistency (halo effect)
Focuses on existing evidence and ignores absent evidence
Computes more than intended (shotgun mentality)
Frames decision problems narrowly, in isolation from one another (silo thinking)
Generates a limited set of basic assessments

CHARACTERISTICS OF SYSTEM TWO THINKING:

In comparison to System 1 thinking, System 2 Thinking requires attention and focus.

Below are some characteristics of System 2 Thinking:

Bracing for the starter gun at a track race
Monitoring the appropriateness of your behavior in a social situation
Checking the validity of a complex logical argument.

In comparing the functions of the right brain and left brain to Kahneman's fast and slow thinking, it appears that System 1 thinking or fast thinking resembles the functions identified in the right brain such as unconscious actions, intuition, emotional quotient, and interpreting information. Whereas, System 2 thinking or slow thinking represents the functions in the left brain such as logical thinking, processing information, and the intelligent quotient.

Kahneman,stated that one of the redeeming qualities of slow thinking is that it can be used to correct fast thinking by identifying the areas that need attention and focus. Kahneman described an association process, where words, ideas, and events become triggers for past experiences. This conditioning process can trigger either negative or positive experiences depending upon what an individual has experienced in their life time. Kahnerman stated that fear can be part the conditioning that a person has learned from their experiences. The brain stores our experiences and our emotional memories.

The next section discusses the amygdala which is the emotional center of the brain. As depicted in the illustrations, the almond shape size of the amygdala is relatively small in comparison to the frontal cortex. However, the purpose for which it was designed has equipped the amygdala with unique properties. One property of the amygdala is its' capacity to send neuro transmitted emotional signals to the brain and throughout the body at a speed of 20 milliseconds as compared to the frontal cortex which processes information at a speed of 300 milliseconds (www.effective mind control.com, 2015). This capacity is linked to the fact that the amygdala is part of the limbic system which is one of the oldest parts of the brain. The illustration below depicts the amygdala within the context of the limbic system.

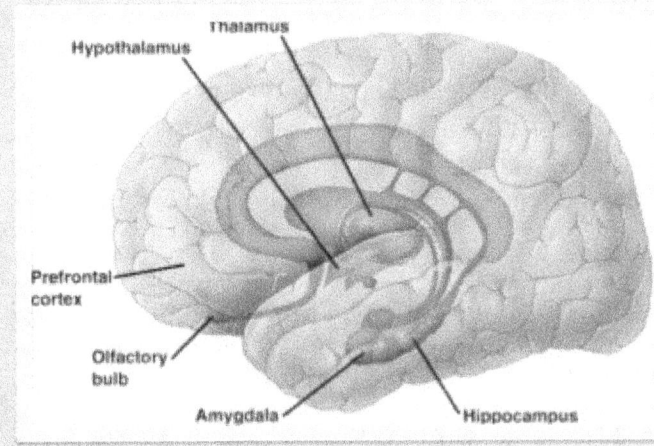

the Limbic System

Thalamus
Hypothalamus
Prefrontal cortex
Olfactory bulb
Amygdala
Hippocampus

* group of structures in the brain, including the amygdala and the hippocampus, that are collectively involved in emotional expression, memory, and motivation.

* amygdala plays an important role in emotion, particularly in response to unpleasant or punishing stimuli

* hippocampus is located in the interior temporal lobes and plays a central role in the storing of new memories, the response to new and unexpected stimuli, and navigational ability

   * plays a role in the brain's internal representation of space in the form of neural maps

Fear and the Amygdala

As part of the oldest part of our brain, "the reptilian brain", the amygdala responds to emotional stimuli that cause fear. The amygdala processes emotional charged stimuli and prepares our body to respond to threats whether they are real or imaginary. In addition to fear, the amygdala influences other emotional dispositions such as aggression, maternal, sexual, and ingestive (eating and drinking) behaviors (LeDoux, 2008). Overall, the amygdala is involved in the following body functions:

- Arousal
- Autonomic Responses Associated with Fear
- Emotional Responses
- Hormonal Secretions
- Memory

In order to help us survive threatening situations, the amygdala engages in a learning process which stores word, ideas, and events that have been associated with some form of adverse consequences that result in pain or discomfort. *Fear conditioning is an associative learning process* by which we learn through repeated experiences to fear something. (Bailey, 2015).

This fear conditioning is similar to the classical conditioning principles that Ivan Pavlov used in conditioning a dog to salivate by ringing a bell. This same principle of social learning occurs within the amygdala when words, things, events, and environments are paired with negative experiences.

In law enforcement, a police officer's amygdala may be triggered by race, war stories, shoot, don't shoot exercises, weapons, the perception of weapons, verbal threats, threats of bodily harm, perceived threats of bodily harm, contempt of cop arrest (Lopez,2011), failure to comply, a macho police culture, an epigenetic inheritance, a bad neighborhood, a dangerous assignment, or *any kind of circumstance where fear can be attached.* In police work, all these circumstances and many more may evoke a sense of fear. Bouton (1988) stated that these learned fear responses may be attenuated by repeated exposure to fear arousing stimulus even in a safe or neutral context (Myers and Davis, 2002). The conditioning of fear arousing stimuli results from association networks and pairing neutral stimuli with learned fear stimuli.

Police officers are trained to handle dangerous situations. So, what levels of fear are considered normal and what levels are considered excessive? Other than the legal and sociological explanations, are there any other possible alternative explanations? It is this query that we hope will start both discussion and dialogue. How do we define and determine an acceptable fear threshold for police officers prior to their employment and periodically during their employment? And more importantly, why should we?

Amygdala Hijack Neuron Pathways

In the first diagram below, after visualizing an emotional stimuli, our brain sends a signal to the thalamus which acts as a relay sensory station. During an amygdala hijack, the emotional signal goes directly from the thalamus to the amygdala. When the thalamus sends emotional signals to the amygdala, these signals are received by fear neurons labelled the lateral, basal, central nuclei, and intercalated cells. The lateral fear neuron(s) is considered the sensory gateway of the amygdala and receives sensory inputs from all our senses (Debiec and LeDoux, 2009). The second diagram describes what happens when the amygdala is hijacked. This diagram illustrates two paths (direct and indirect). The indirect path is where a neural signal goes to the frontal cortex for processing. In comparison, the direct path represents the path taken when the amygdala is hijacked. Some researchers label the direct path of an amygdala hijack as the low road and indirect path as the high road (frontal cortex).

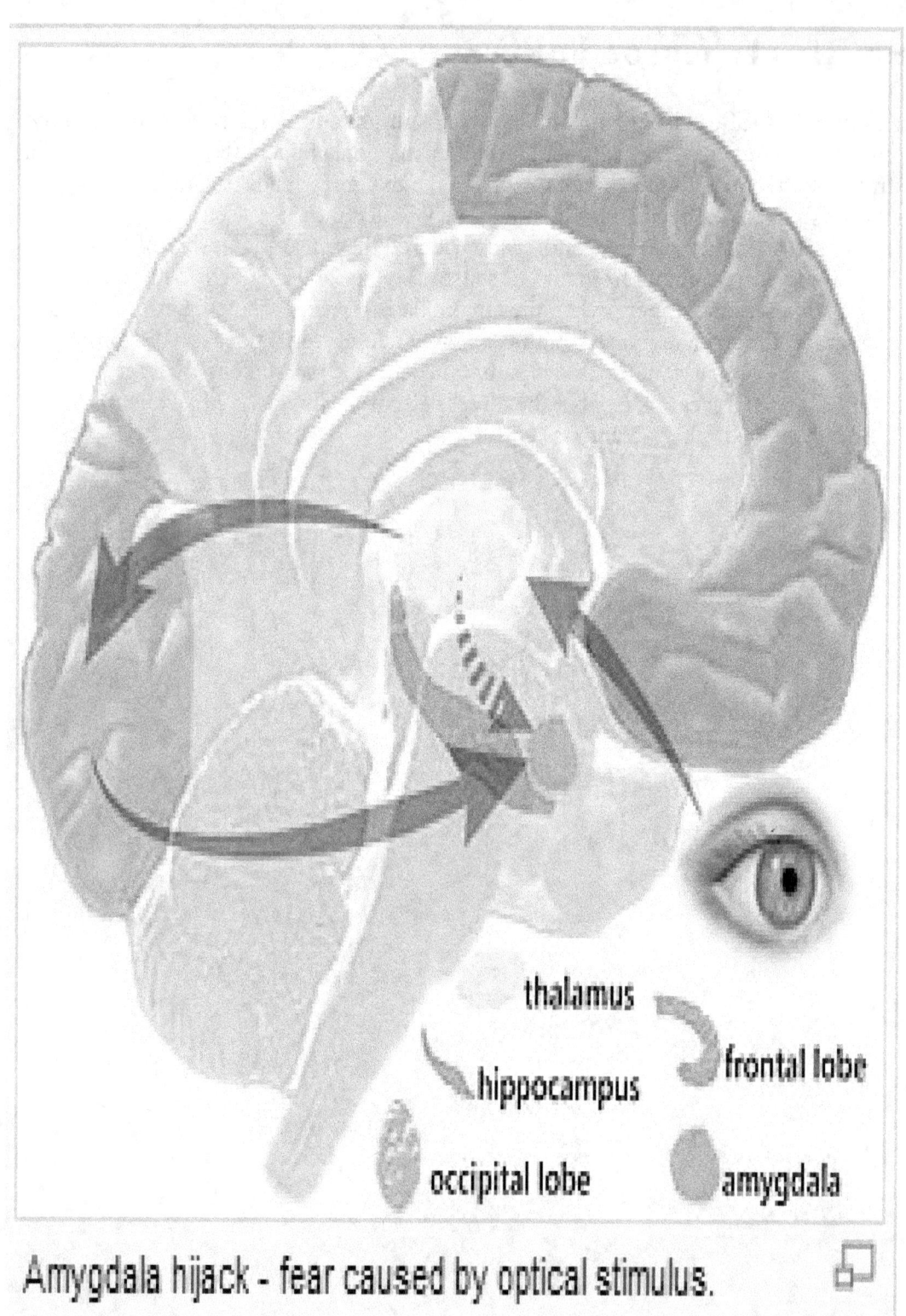

thalamus

hippocampus

frontal lobe

occipital lobe

amygdala

Amygdala hijack - fear caused by optical stimulus.

AMYGDALA HIJACK (Diagram 2)

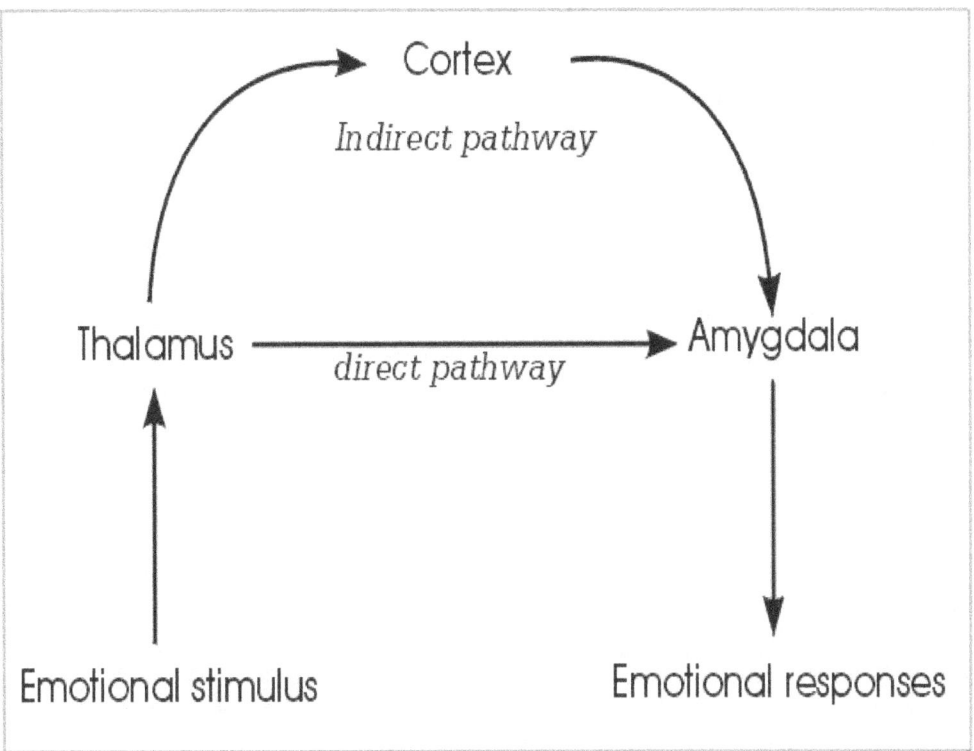

Fig 1: *Direct and indirect pathways to the amygdala.*

Source: J. LeDoux, *The Emotional Brain* (Phoenix (an Imprint of The Orion Publishing Group), London, 1999) as cited in Rimmele (2003).

According to Rimmele (2003), the trade- off between an emotional stimulus taking the direct path over the indirect path is that the direct path provides a cruel incomplete representation of the stressful or fearful situation. In contrast, the indirect route takes longer but provides a more accurate assessment of the situation. From the perspective of the officer who is concerned with officer safety, time can be the different between life and death. However, from the perspective of a grieving loved one, a delay in the officer's actions to gather more information regarding the situation is the preferred action to take. Life threatening events can occur within the blink of an eye; therefore, neuroscience training must be provided before events escalate. This is a form of proactive policing.

As mentioned, the amygdala takes about 20 milliseconds to react to threatening stimuli while the frontal cortex takes about 300 milliseconds to react (www.effective mind control.com, The Amygdala & Emotions-Effective Mind Control, Oct. 19, 2015).

In order to achieve a win –win outcomes, police confrontations require integrating and balancing the concerns of the police for officer safety and the concerns of a possible grieving mother as a joint condition for building trust between the police and the community. This training can help to defuse confrontations before they become deadly. Because individuals have differ experiences (mental models and mental maps); our perception and our interpretation of what we see or hear may be different for each individual. These differences in how we perceive danger applies to both police and citizens. While this balancing act presents a challenge, it can also be used as an opportunity to improve police and community relations.

ALMYGDALA HIJACK ACTIVATES THE SYMPATHETIC NERVOUS SYSTEM

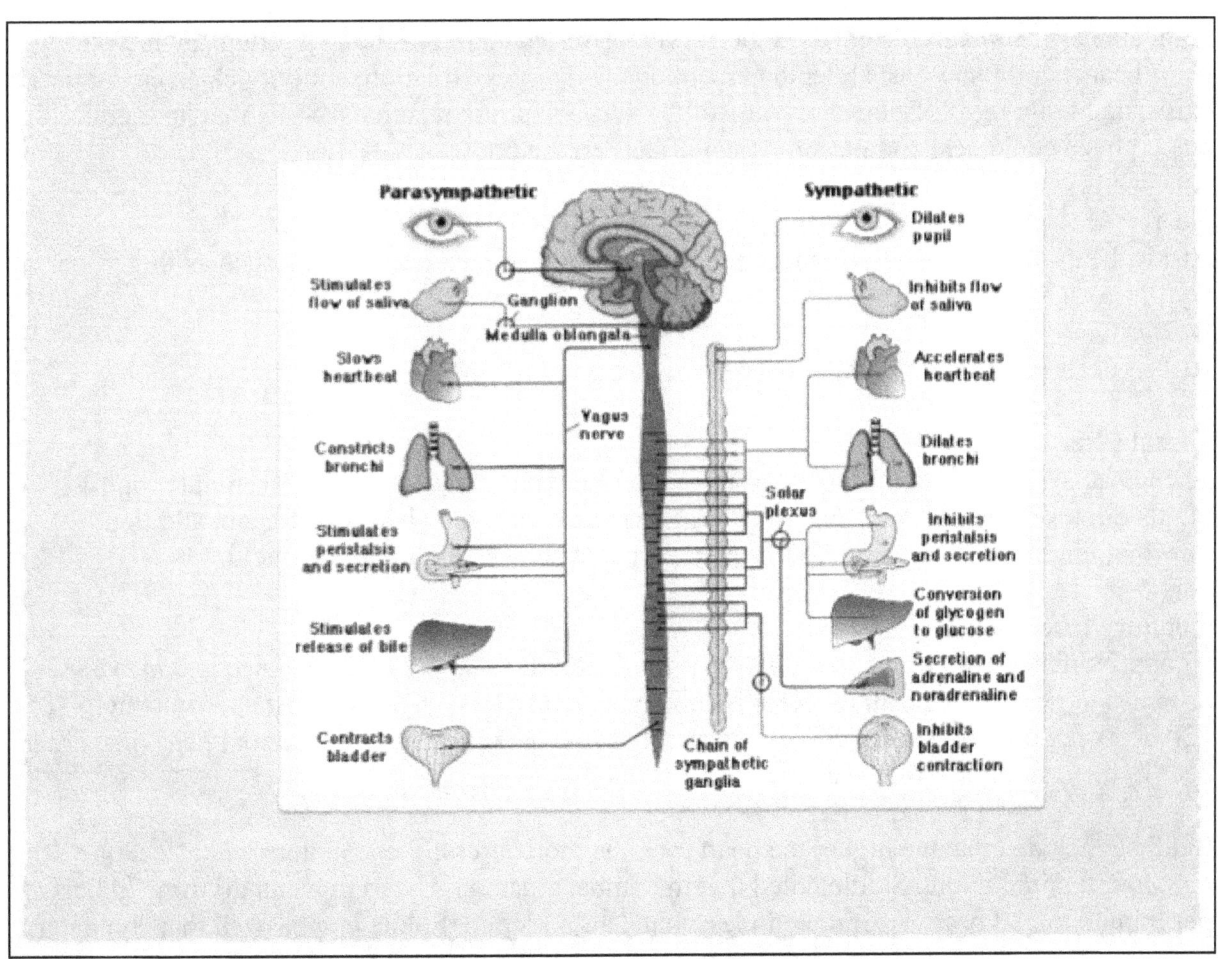

THE SYMPATHETIC NERVOUS SYSTEM HIJACKS DE-ESCALATION TRAINING

The fear conditioning and fear processing areas of the brain are located in the phylogenetically structures commonly known as the "reptilian brain". The amygdala is part of our "reptilian brain". During an amygdala hijack, the sympathetic nervous system is activated. The above chart identifies physiological changes that take place during an amygdala hijack: pupil dilation, inhibiting flow of saliva, accelerated heartbeat, dilated bronchi, conversion of glycogen to glucose, secretion of adrenalin, and inhibited bladder contraction. *In most cases, the hard wiring of our brain during an amygdala hijack can negate police training.*

IMPACT OF AMYGDALA HIJACK ON VITAL ORGANS

In his book, Sharpening The Warrior's Edge, Bruce Siddle (1995), discussed what happens to the body during combat situations. He based his initial research on how soldiers performed under stress. Siddle compared the sympathetic nervous system effect on vital organs to non-combatants. His research compared the survival stress reaction of the two groups by measuring heart beats per minute, visual depth perception changes, eye dilation, auditory changes, motor skills, and brain recall. Below are some of the survival stress reactions (SSR) that he found. SSR has both psychological and physiological effects on the body:

Heart
At 115 beats per minute (bpm), most people lose line complex motor skills such as finger.

Dexterity.
At 145 beats per minute (bpm), most people lose complex motor skills.

Visual Effects
The visual system is the primary sensory organ of the body. At 175 beats per minute (bpm), pupils dilate and flatten resulting into *"tunnel vision"*. A person backs up to gain addition information on the threat. Studies cite a 70 percent decrease in their visual field.

Auditory Effects
At approximately 145 beats per minute (bpm), that part of *the brain shuts down and hearing becomes difficult.* The recall problem is called "Critical Stress Amnesia". At approximately 185-220 beats per minute (bpm), individuals may become paralyzed, show irrational behavior, or the deer in the headlights syndrome.

Siddle concluded that the higher the heart rate, the more stressful encounters will affect one's *perception of the threat*. Siddle noted that in combat a person's heart rate can go from 70 beats per minute to 220 beats per minute in less than half a second. Siddle emphasized that combatants who are able to keep their heart rate between 115 to 145 beats per minute are still capable of performing adequately. This research on stress testing can be used as a metric in the use of force and de-escalation training and testing. The following section reflects the comments by several neuroscience experts on areas related to neuroscience research that trainers may consider in developing their de-escalation and use of force practices.

NARRATIVE BY NEUROSCIENCE EXPERTS

Neuroscience can serve as a resource for officers and citizens in understanding themselves and how their brain works under stress/fear. As part of a *community outreach strategy*, neuroscience research can reduce critical incidents, domestic disputes, and police confrontations. The following excerpts are from neuroscience researchers on a variety but related topics.

Culture and Mental Maps:

Rock and Schwartz (2006) stated that professionals in different functions — finance, operations, legal, marketing, and so forth — literally think with different neurological connections. **Rock and Schwartz (2006) stated that our brain reconfigures itself both chemically and physically based on what we focus on**. Rock and Schwartz (2006), further stated that prolonged attention on an experience can shape not only our mental map(s) but also our personality. This point seems relevant to how the police culture can influence how an officer perceives the world around him and influences how he or she behaves.

Amygdala Hijack

LeDoux (1999) and Rimmele (2003) described what happens to the brain and the body when encountering a stressful or fearful situation. In normal situations, information is processed by the cortex, the largest portion of the brain. However, when the brain is alerted that danger exist, it sends a chemical signal to the amygdala (the size of a peanut) for a fight or flight response. Rimmele (2003), stated that a trade- off exist when a direct path to the amygdala is taken versus an indirect path to the frontal cortex. **When the emotional stimulus takes a direct path to the amygdala, a cruel and incomplete representation of the fearful situation is perceived**. In comparison, the indirect route allows for more time to gather information and results in a more accurate assessment of the situation.

Toxic Thoughts

With respect to our thinking, Dr. Leaf, (2013) stated that negative thinking contributes anywhere from 75 to 98 percent of our mental, physical, and behavioral illness. This staggering and eye-opening statistic means only 2 to 25 percent of mental and physical illnesses come from the environment and genes. Dr. Leaf states that how we think affects us both physically and emotionally. **Our thinking acts as a switch which is capable of turning on either negative or positive genes.** She admonishes us that we need to take control of our thought process in order to change our health and behavior.

Stress Training and DNA

Southwick and Charney (2012) stated that there are some applicable limitations on stress training based on similar research with soldiers. Each officer has an emotional history and DNA that may cause them to respond differently to a stressful confrontation and/or event. **These researchers further stated that our ability to adapt and cope successfully differs based on a complex set of outcomes, which include genetic, biological, psychological, social and spiritual factors.** What makes one officer shoot well under stress and another drop his gun is based on individual difference(s). These individual differences revert back to the unique set of experiences that a person has been exposed to or not exposed to.

Experimental Thinking versus Rational Thinking

Seymour Epstein (1994) is a noted researcher in the area of stress and fear. In his research, he differentiate between rational thinking and experimental thinking. He described "rational thinking" as occurring during situations where the individual experiences low emotional arousal whereas "experiential thinking" takes place when emergency situations occurs. Like Kahneman's concept of fast thinking, Epstein defined experiential thinking as thinking that is, "automatically, rapidly, effortlessly, and efficiently processes of information.". **Epstein pointed out that in stressful encounters *"experiential thinking" is dominant over the rational system* because it requires less effort, its' more efficient, and, is the default option, as cited in Artwohl (2008).**

Epstein (1994) further stated that experiential thinking informs us of the following:

1) **Experiential thinking is based on *past experiences*.** This means that under sudden, life threatening stress, some behavior will likely pop up automatically without conscious thought, and the officer and the community can only hope that those past experiences will include up to date training that has programmed an effective and appropriate response. This means not only training officers *in appropriate tactics, but also providing sufficient repetition under stress* so that the new behaviors will take precedent over any previously learned, potentially inappropriate, behaviors they brought with them to the job (Hume, 1992), as cited in Epstein (1994).

2) "Experientially derived knowledge is often more compelling and more likely to influence behavior than is abstract knowledge." This is especially critical in sudden, high stress, physical performance based situations. Abstract knowledge obtained in lectures and books can be very useful for "rational thinking" low stress situations such as *formulating policies, analyzing situations, etc.*

3) Reality based training (scenario based training) subjects police to high levels of stress, and will help officers *develop coping mechanisms to compensate for the perceptual and memory distortions.* To compensate for tunnel vision, many officers and soldiers have learned to practice "visually scanning" the tactical environment during high stress situations, as cited by Epstein in Artwohl (2008).

4) Epstein (1994) also mentioned that it is important to utilize the functions of our total brain. He stated that our failure in synthesizing the functions of our brain can result in habitual responses, especially under stress. As previous mentioned, Epstein's work served as research for Kahneman (2011) two model systems labelled fast thinking (system 1) and slow thinking (system 2). Both Epstein's experimental thinking and Kahneman's fast thinking are predicated on the hard wiring of the "reptilian brain".

World Views

Boyatzis, Rochford, and Taylor (2015) distinguished between positive and negative views. **The positive views were energized by positive emotions and were referred to as promotion focus. The negative views were fueled by negative emotions such as fear, guilt, anxiety, shame, and defensiveness.** These world views or mental maps reflect our experiences. Police officers also develop mental maps and world views that sometimes unconsciously impact their personality and their performance. Neuroscience can be used to help police and citizens better understand each other's world views, manage stress levels, and promote dialogue. The next section examines how neuroscience research can be applied to scenario based training.

The ABC's of Emotions

The above references converge on an individual's belief system or world view. Dr. Albert Ellis, (1980) renowned psychologist, distinguished between emotions and feelings. In explaining, he reasoned that our emotional reaction to an event is not really about the event but our belief about that event. This is a crucial piece of information with respect to statements that *I was in fear of my life.* According to Dr. Ellis, the letter A represents the activating event, the letter B represents the belief held about the event, and letter C represents the emotional consequences as a result of our belief(s). The letter B represents our belief and our feeling about that event. Ellis believes our feeling about an event is what influences our choice of emotions. So if an officer believes or feels that an event will result in harm; then, he or she acquires an emotion to support that belief. In this case, the emotion is fear. The choice that one has in believing that an event can or may result into a negative consequence rather than a positive outcome depends upon the belief system of that individual officer. This concern, however, must be met with extreme caution because an officer can easily engage in a self-fulling prophecy where **his predictions or his expectations of the outcome are used to influence the officer's behavior in making the outcome true.** So the concern becomes, is it possible that an officer can approach an event with a predisposition and that predisposition influences the actions taken by that officer. If so, neuroscience testing could determine the officer's belief system or predisposition to events prior to critical incidents. In the next section, the author discusses how neuroscience could be integrated into shoot, don't shoot exercises.

IN-SERVICE SHOOT, DON'T SHOOT TRAINING RECCOMENDATIONS

In the United States, there are over 18,000 police departments. Because each may have a different method of training, the author is making only generic suggestions. In terms of scenario based training, one of the most common scenario based training exercises is the **Shoot, Don't Shoot exercise**. In the previous section on survival stress training, Siddle (1995) suggested the importance of keeping the heart rate within a range of 115 to 145 beats per minute in order to performance adequately. Laur (2002) recommended attention and focus be given to the following areas:

> Skill Confidence
> Stimulus Response Training based on real experiences
> Visualization (short term memory)
> Breathing (autogenic breathing)
> Value of Life
> Training
> Average reaction time to one stimulus is one second.
> Multiple responses to the same threat stimuli confuses the brain with choices and results in a delayed response (that may be the different between life or death).
> Training should be taught in partitions and repetition.

In addition to these areas, this author believes police trainers should incorporate a neuroscience research design to measure and evaluate Shoot, Don't Shoot exercises. This would provide empirical research that could be used as baseline data in defining and determining fear threshold standards that could possibly result in some form of "best practices". In order to implement such a research design using neuroscience metrics, the following suggestions are offered as a blueprint:

> Before and after heart beats per minute examines taken for each officer participating in the shoot, don't shoot exercise in order to establish a biometric baseline database..
>
> Heart beats per minute examination taken after each field shooting or excessive force incident as close to the time of the shooting occurrence as possible.
>
> Semi-annual comparison of in-service exercise data to field data for training purposes.
>
> Interview of officer, using the Los Angeles Police Department's totality of circumstances checklist, after field shooting or excessive force incident(s).
>
> Document perceptual distortions in the reporting of shooting or excessive force incidents.
>
> Develop "best practices" based on empirical evidence gathered from critical incidents, shooting, and excessive force incidents.

Maintain documented reports of perceptual distortions made by officers in the above incidents as part of the officer's performance evaluation file.

Research changes in biometrics when testing officers on word association exercises that may trigger the amygdala and may result in negative behavior.

These recommendations to integrate neuroscience in the existing use of force and de-escalation training programs are not a panacea. They are suggestions that may or may not reduce the number of shooting and use of force incidents in a particular department. This author understands that adult learners require a diverse array of training material to reinforce learning. Therefore, this author prescribes a holistic training approach. The notion that one size fits all is not truth, erroneous, misleading, and ineffective. Throughout this book, from neuroscience, to shoot, don't shoot, to implicit bias, a common denominator that connects each component of this book is *the life experiences of the people involved. The assumption that we all think the same way and act the same way is so misleading. The training is aimed at* self-development. The training includes both intra-personal and inter-personal human development strategies that will enhance an individual's growth as a citizen and or as a police personnel. *These training strategies are provided based on the premise that when we feel good about who we are, we built our own capacity to care for others.*

CHAPTER FIVE   PROACTIVE HOLISTIC TRAINING

This chapter addresses the importance of personal development. In addition to neuroscience, it offers strategies in: transactional analysis, emotional intelligence, system thinking, Covey's talking stick, and procedural justice. These strategies can be used in an outreach capacity with the community as well as with the police to build trust and improve police community relations.

PROACTIVE HOLISTIC TRAINING

TRANSACTIONAL ANALYSIS (Harris, 1967)

Transactional Analysis (TA) is a personality model that consist of three components: parent, child, and adult. It can be used to evaluate an officer or citizen's background for learned prejudices and expose **negative life experiences**. While each individual possesses these same three components, their personalities differs based on their DNA, parental rearing, the environment, education, and life experiences. This component can help individuals identify self-esteem issues, trust issues, and racial biases as learned behavior. It can also provide clues to what experiences influenced a person's mental map. The parent component of the model represents rules and dogma that one is socialized to at home or at work. The child represents our dual emotional tendencies of playfulness and sadness. And lastly, our adult component represents our real time computer that analyzes and deletes obsolete information, rules and emotional baggage. TA is a self-assessment tool that can help us understand why we behavior the way we do.

EMOTIONAL INTELLIGENCE (Goleman, 1998)

Today, most police department incorporate some type of emotional intelligence training. Emotional Intelligence training focuses on four areas: a) self- awareness, b) self- regulation, c) social awareness, and d) relationship management. Emotional Intelligence (EI) places a strong emphasis on empathy in order to understand the views, attitudes, and behavior of another individual. In fact, neuroscience research describe the brain's using mirror neurons to understand the emotional state that another human being is experiencing. The term **amygdala hijack** was coined by Goleman. Police see people when they are most vulnerable; EI provides individuals with the knowledge and skills to de-escalate emotional charged situations. Citizens and police can benefit from EI training because it teaches self-control.

SYSTEM THINKING (Senge,1990)

System thinking is a holistic approach to solving problems that intersect multiple disciplines. Framing a problem with a fraction of its parts only results in partial solutions. Senge suggested the following communication strategies to address our unconscious thinking below the surface. He opined that our hidden assumptions can influence how we framed and attempted to solve problems without our knowing. As problem solving and relationship building mechanism, Senge (1990) suggested the following strategies: dialog, suspending judgment, leaps of abstraction, exposing the left hand column, balancing inquiry with advocacy, and espouse theory versus theory in use.

Leaps of Abstraction occurs when an individual makes a single observation and uses the observation to make generalization(s).

Exposing the left hand column is a concept that addresses the notion that we are not consciously aware of all our assumptions at a given time. As such, what may influence a particular decision may be hidden from us. Exposing the left hand is a method which forces us to identify with what we didn't say out loud but may have been thinking. Senge hinted that when we deliberately hide information; then, we don't have any intentions on solving a problem.

Most organizations use a debate format to discuss matters. Balancing inquiry with advocacy is a format where critical thinking and sharing one's assumptions with others enhance problem solving when information is freely exchanged and synthesized.

Espoused Theory v. Theories in Use represents the gaps between what we say versus what we do. Discovering gaps in policies, procedures, and behaviors lead to improvements and long terms goal achievement. In retrospect, many officers suggested that the training that they received in the academy was devalued once they hit the street. Espouse theories versus theories in use is a comparative means of measuring the integrity of an organization, group, or leader.

COVEY'S TALKING STICK (COMMUNICATION FACILITATOR)

The talking stick is a concept borrowed from the Native Indians. In fact, it was the first form of procedural justice. The idea was to create an atmosphere where everyone had an opportunity to address the Council and the talking stick was used as a procedural protocol tool to facilitate inclusiveness by allowing everyone the opportunity to be heard. Dialogue, rather than discussion, was facilitated by requesting the talking stick from the speaker only after the listener clearly understood and verified what the speaker meant by repeating it. The conversation did not end until both parties understood one another. This communication strategy can be used to addresses implicit bias, transparency, hidden assumptions, and our mental models (Covey, 1989). This communication strategy builds trust.

PROCEDURAL JUSTICE

Procedural justice theory is no longer a novelty in law enforcement. Procedural justice is characterized by employee input, fair treatment, respectfulness, and value recognition. Procedural justice research has shown that outcomes are accepted even if the disposition was unfavorable when parties perceive the process to be fair (Lind andTyler, 1988). According to PERF (2014), procedural justice can be defined in terms of four issues. This author list two of the four: a) people want the opportunity to tell their side of the story and b) the public is concern with an officer's intentions, just as much as an officer's skills. Below are two cases that illustrate the important of a procedural justice process:

In case one, a class-action suit brought by Hispanic drivers in Maricopa County, Arizona, alleged that police deputies under the leadership of Sheriff Joe Arpaio were **illegally using race as grounds to stop**, detain, and arrest the occupants of vehicles. In May 2013, a federal judge ruled that the patrols had indeed "incorporated race as a consideration into their operations," and banned Sheriff Arpaio's unfair operating procedures [8], as cited by (Gaynor, 2013), in Maiese (2013).

In case two, the U.S. District Court ruled on August 12, 2013, that NYPD's stop and frisk practices violated the Constitutional rights of members of minority groups. U.S. District Judge Shira A. Sheindlin's stated: "I emphasize at the outset, as I have throughout the litigation that this case is not about the effectiveness of stop and frisk in deterring or combating crime. This Court's mandate is solely to judge the *constitutionality of police behavior*, not its effectiveness as a law enforcement tool." Many police practices may be useful for fighting crime — preventive detention or coerced confessions, for example — but because they are unconstitutional they cannot be used, no matter how effective. While it is true that any one stop is a limited intrusion in duration and deprivation of liberty, each stop can also be a demeaning and humiliating experience. *No one should live in fear* of being stopped whenever he leaves his home to go about the activities of daily life. Those who are routinely subjected to stops are overwhelmingly people of color, and they are justifiably troubled to be singled out when many of them have done nothing to attract the unwanted attention. Some plaintiffs testified that stops make them feel unwelcome in some parts of the City, and *distrustful of the police*. This alienation cannot be good for the police, the community, or its leaders. Fostering trust and confidence between the police and the community would be an improvement for everyone (New York Times, 2013).

The above cases are not only relevant from a procedural justice standpoint but it also emphasizes that fear is a two way street and some *citizens' fear the police*. As illustrated in these two procedural justice cases, a tainted process can condition the public to fearing the police as much as a gun can put fear in a policeman. Overall, the accumulated effect of developing these human development strategies is to improve the interactive/relationship process between police and citizens and to rebuild workable levels of trust between police and community members.

The above self-development strategies are based on the premise that both police and citizens can improve who they are. But more important, this training does not separate the individual from the environment that he or she lives or works in. Therefore, the environmental forces and the conditions that people live under must be taken in account in understanding their world view. The above training strategies provide some workable tools for improving ones' self and ones' relationship with others. The next section offers a summation of the author's concerns.

CHAPTER SIX   CONCLUSION

CONCLUSION

In the past, there has been a number of explanations for the disproportionate number of police shooting in minority neighborhoods. Without choosing one explanation over any other, this author agrees with most police officers that fear is a dominant motivator when officers are concerned about their safety. While police are trained to deal with fear, there are incidents where fear overrides rational thinking and compliance with department policies. This is possible because our bodies are hard wired a certain way.

As a basic survival instinct, our bodies reacts to fear by engaging the sympathetic nervous system and the amygdala. The amygdala is a protective reflex that protects the body from harm. Where a person is threaten with danger, the amygdala engages in a fight or flight response. The amygdala is part of the body's self-governing mechanism. While police officers can benefit from neuroscience research, so can citizens. Some of the most deadly calls for police, involve domestic violence situations. For citizens, it might include road rage. As such, neuroscience can also help citizens understand how their brain works under fear. Acquiring neuroscience knowledge may enable us to make a split second decision that may be the difference between life or death. This knowledge can be useful for police as well as citizens. *Neuroscience can be used by police departments as a form of community outreach.*

Neuroscientist has informed us that fear can be subjective and interpreted differently by each person (police or citizen). Therefore, each individual has a different fear threshold. Defining a fear threshold is significant in policing because it sets a standard for who is qualified to handle the various fears associated with the job. Neuroscience informs us …..that our levels of fear intensify every time we experience similar emotional stimuli. In other words, the emotions that we experienced during a negative event are relived every time a similar events occurs. Police deal with negative events daily. At present, we have no way of knowing how an individual officer or citizen is affected by fear.

Currently, we have a pre-employment psychological screening test. This test is focused on the personality traits of a police officer that center around ethical behavior. These test may address personality traits that include: honesty, judgment, general intelligence, lack of bias, impulse control, or the ability to tolerate stress (Roufa, 2017). Most of these test are multiple choice in nature and do not focus on the totality of an officer's fear related experiences. As mentioned, these test are concern with the overall character of a police officer and what character issues may impact performance. The current pre-employment psychological screening test does not help us predict what words, ideas, things, or situations may trigger an amygdala hijack as it relates to police shooting or de-escalation practices. The absence of such an assessment tool contributes to what seems to be a universal response after a shooting that *I was in fear of my life.* Without any neuroscience test to establish acceptable fear parameters or thresholds, this response will unfortunately continue. It is this void that this author is concern with. How do we train to manage fear, measure fear, and identify acceptable fear levels? Responding to this void is not only beneficial to the police for hiring and retention purposes but also to avoid municipal liability. Neuroscience testing can fill this void.

Incorporating neuroscience research within the use of force and de-escalation training could help **define and determine acceptable fear thresholds for police recruits and for season veterans**. In the military, jet pilots are subject to stress test to determine whether or not they can cope with g-forces. Neuroscience research could be used in the same capacity. Determining an officer's fear threshold may be more important than body cams, batons, guns, athletic built, Tasers, and etc. because when fear levels are uncontrollable, rational thinking and policy compliance are overridden. A course in neuroscience aimed at lowering excessive force incidents would pay huge dividends in building trust between the police and the communities they serve. Under high fear levels, individuals are said to experience tunnel vision where factually neutral information is distorted. *This distortion can be the different between life and death.*

Neuroscience research is a proactive training strategy aimed at determining an officer's capacity to manage fear. **In essence, it explains how fear impacts an officer's performance**. Neuroscience assures citizens that police administrators are doing everything in their power to improve police community relations and are continuously looking for more ways of building trust within all communities. In closing, neuroscience along with the other proposed holistic training recommendations are strategies for mending the mistrust between police and citizens. Again, these holistic training strategies can be used as a form of community outreach. *By shifting the narrative from* implicit bias, judicial case standards, procedural justice, crisis intervention, and cultural diversity *to neuroscience research*, this author believes understanding how the brain works aligns itself with the testimony given by officers who were or have been engaged in a police shooting that they were *"in fear of their life"*. Neuroscience research and testing answers not just, *what is going* on but the *why its' going on*. It also offers a concrete scientific solution, supported by empirical evidence.

This author believes that it would be encouraging for the Department of Justice and/or local police agencies to commit resources: a) to develop a course in neuroscience research in conjunction with de-escalation and use of force training and b) to develop an neuroscience fear assessment tool to remove officers or reassign officers who lack a capacity to manage their fear within acceptable levels.

OUR GREATEST GLORY IS NOT IN NEVER FALLING,

BUT IN RISING EVERY TIME WE FALL (CONFUCIOUS).

REFERENCES:

Artwohl, A. & Christensen. L. (1997). *Deadly Force Encounters: What a Cops Need to Know to Mentally and Physically Prepare for and Win a Gunfight.* Boulder, CO: Paladin Press.

Ax, J. and Polansek, T. (2015). Chicago Cop's Defense in Murder Case Depends on His Fears, Extent of Threat, *Neuters*, Nov. 25, 2015.

Bailey, CH, Kandel, ER, Harris, KM, (2015). *Structural components of synaptic plasticity and memory consolidation.* Cold Spring Harbor Laboratory Press

Bouton, M.E. (1988). Context and ambiguity in the extinction of emotional learning: implications for exposure therapy. *Behav Res. Ther* 26, 137-49.

Boyatizis, R.E., Rochford, K., & Taylor, S. N. (2015). The role of the positive emotional attractor in vision and shared vision: toward effective leadership, relationships, and engagement, *Front Psychology*, 6:670

Campbell, J. (1990), *The Improbable Machine*, Touchstone Books

Chamine, S., (2015). *Positive Intelligence*, Greenleaf Book Group Press, Austin, Texas.

Covey, S.R.. (1989). *The Seven Habits of Highly Effective People: Restoring the Character Ethic,* Simon and Schuster, Inc. New York, New York.

Crimesider (2017). *White St. Louise Police Officer Shoots Off-Duty Black Officer*, Staff CBS News June 23, 2017, 3:55 PM.

Debiec, Jacek. and LeDoux, Joseph. (2009). *The Amygdala and Neural Pathways of Fear.* In Shiromani, P. ; Keane, T. ; LeDoux, J.E. (eds), (2009), Post-Traumatic Stress Disorder: Basic Science and Clinical Practice, 428p., Humana Press, doi: 10.1007/978-1-60327-329-9_2

Ellis, A. (1980). *Rational Emotive Self-Help Techniques*. New York: BMA.

Epstein, S. (1994). Integration of the cognitive and the psychodynamic unconscious. *American Psychologist*, 49, 709-724.

Gaynor, T. & Schwartz, D. "Arizona Sheriff Joe Arpaio Racially Profiled Latinos, Federal Judge Rules." *Reuters*. May 25, 2013. <http://www.huffingtonpost.com/2013/05/24/arpaio-racialprofiling_n_3333907.html>.

Goleman, D. (1998). *Working with Emotional Intelligence*. Bantam Books. New York

Graham v. Connor, 490 U.S. 386 (1989)

Harris, T. A. (2004). *I'm OK, You're OK*. Harper Row

Kahneman, D. (2011). *Thinking, Fast and Slow*. Farrar, Strauss, Giroux, New York.

Laur, D. (2002). *The anatomy of fear and how it relates to survival skills training*. Retrieved on 10-14-2013 from http://www.lwcbooks.com/articles/anatomy.html

Leaf, C., (2013). *Switch on Your Brain*, Grand Rapids, MI. Baker Books Publishing

LeDoux, J. (1999). *The Emotional Brain* (Phoenix , an Imprint of The Orion Publishing Group), London, 1999) as cited in Rimmele (2003).

LeDoux, J. (2008). *Emotional networks and motor control: a fearful view*, Center for Neural Science, 6 Washington Place, New York University, New York.

Le Doux, J.E. and Phelps, E.A. and (2005). Contributions of the Amygdala to Emotion Processing: From Animal Models to Human Behavior. *Neuron,* Volume 48, Issue 2, 20 October 2005, pages 175-187.

Lind, E.A. & Tyler, T. R. (1988). *The Social Psychology of Procedural Justice*. New York, New York: Plenum.

Lopez, C.E. (2010). *"Disorderly (mis) Conduct: The Problem with Contempt of Cop'Arrest,"* Issue Brief, American Constitution Society (Washington, D.C.:2010), available at: www.acslaw.org/sites/default/files/lopez_Contempt_of_Cop.pdf

Los Angeles Police Department (2015), *Use of Force: End of Year Review Summary*

Lowery, W., (July 11, 2016), The Washington Post (2016), *Aren't more white people than black people killed by police" Yes, but no.*

Maiese, M. . *"Procedural Justice." Beyond Intractability*. Eds. Guy Burgess and Heidi Burgess. Conflict Information Consortium, University of Colorado, Boulder. Posted: January 2004 <http://www.beyondintractability.org/essay/procedural-justice>.

Myers, K.M., and Davis, M. (2002). Behavioral and neural analysis of extinction. *Neuron* 36, 567-84.

Menkes, J. (2005). *Executive Intelligence*. Harper Collins Publishers, LLC. New York, New York.

PERF Summit in Washington, DC. In February 2012 on *Integrated Approach to De-escalation and Minimizing Use of Force*

President's Task Force on 21st Century Policing, Phoenix, AZ, February 14, 2015). PERF Executive Forum 2015 President Obama Task Force 2016

Revlin, R., Leirer, V., and Yopp, H., (1980). "The Belief Bias Effect in Formal Reasoning: The Influence of Knowledge on Logic", *Memory and Cognition*, 8, pp. 584-592.

Roufa, T. (2017). Psychological Tests and Screening for Police Officers, *The Balance.*

U. Rimmele, G. Domes, M. K., H. M., *Neuroreport* , A Primer on Emotions and Learning, 14, 2485-2488 (2003).

Rock, D. & Schwartz, J. (2006). *The Neuroscience of Leadership.* Strategy and Business Magazine, New York, New York. www.strategyand.pwc.com

SCOTUS - https://medium.com/coffee-house-writers/provocation-rule-rejected-5d0ae6b289ea, *Supreme Court Says Cops Justified Even When Provoking A Shooting,* retrieved on 6-19-17.

Senge, Peter. 1990. *The Fifth Discipline: the Art and Practice of the Learning Organization.* New York: Doubleday.

Siddle, B.K. (1995). *Sharpening the Warriors Edge: The Psychology and Science of Training.*

Southwick, S.M. , and Charney, D.S. (2012*). Resilience: the science of mastering life's greatest challenge.* Cambridge University Press.

Thomson, Helen (2015). *Study of Holocaust survivors finds trauma passed on the children's genes.* Retrieved from www.theguardian.com/science , Friday, August 21, 2015.

Wells-Wallace, B. (2016), New York Times, *The Fear Defense: Police Shooting*

www.nytimes.com/2013/08/13/nyregion/stop-and-frisk-practice-violated-rights-judge-rules.html, retrieved on September 15, 2016.

www.mind control.com, The Amygdala & Emotions-Effective Mind Control, Oct. 19, 2015), retrieved on September 15, 2016.

Wikipedia.org//wiki/Bona_fide_occupation qualification, retrieved on June 10, 2017

Wikipedia.org/Wiki/Howard_Morgan_case, 2005

Yehuda, R., Daskalakis, N.P., Bierer, L.M., Bader, H.N., Klengel, T., Holsboer, F., and Binder, E.B. (2015). Holocaust Exposure Induced Intergenerational Effects on FKBP5 Methylation. Biological Psychiatry, *A Journal of Psychiatric Neuroscience and Therapeutics.*

APPENDIX:

THE CEREBRUM

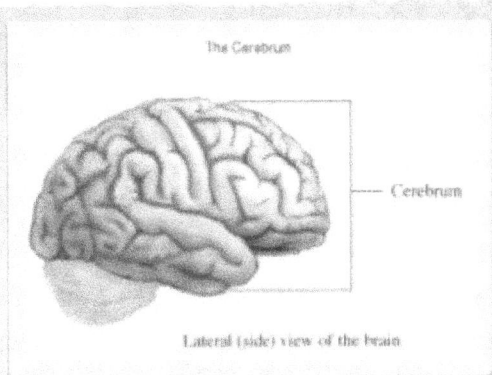

the cerebrum

Lateral (side) view of the brain

* most essential part of the brain is the cerebrum & its cortex

* cerebrum is the largest structure in human brain. it is composed of two cerebral hemisphere, the left & right which control movement & feeling on the opposing side of the body

* corpus callosum connects the two hemisphere and makes possible the transfer of information and the coordination of activity between them

* cerebral cortex is the thin gray outer covering about 1/8 inch thick. it is primarily responsible for the higher mental processes of language, memory & thinking

the thalamus & hypothalamus

* thalamus has two egg-shaped parts, serves as relay station for virtually all the information that flows into and out of the forebrain, including sensory information from all the senses except smell

* hypothalamus regulates hunger, thirst, sexual behavior, and a wide variety of emotional behaviors, and internal body temperature

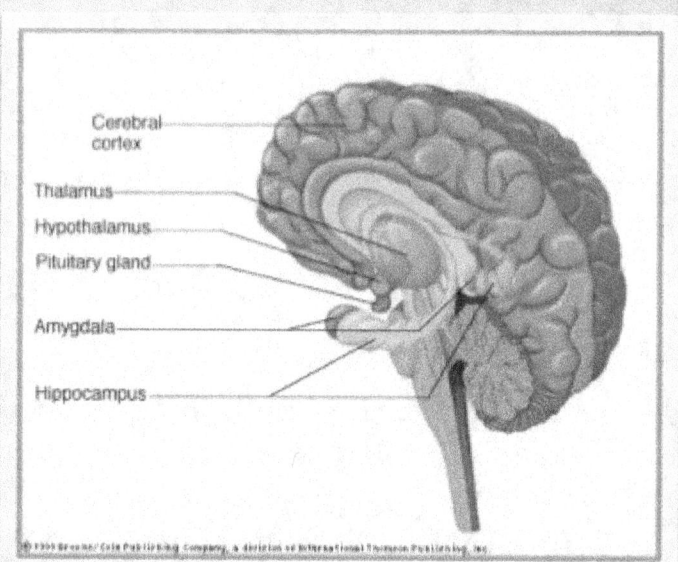